running out of fear

by

bradley f koetting

RUNNING OUT OF FEAR by Bradley F. Koetting

Single Malt Press

PO Box 34

Timberon, NM 88350-0034

bfkoetting@gmail.com

cover photo by sofie marie

Also by Bradley F. Koetting: *fisher of men,*
push buttons and stir pots

ISBN - 978-0-615-26189-8

ACKNOWLEDGMENTS

i'd like to thank God
and all my teammates

for mom

"...there ain't no money in poetry
that's what sets a poet free
and i've had all the freedom i can stand..."

- Guy Clark

'Cold Dog Soup'

entrails

growth
salt cedar
trying
fade
atheists
selfish
interstice
first
hostage
out
pie
fuck me
plenty
110 percent
recovery
same
early
eight
jogging
good
juice
Welch's
years
waiting
welcome
unctuous dick
out here
Paco
depression
twenty
hell
fool's luck
care
my marriage
goats
looky here
my dying dog
curious
rad
a baseball thing
church clothes

warning
why i am such a pussy
control
things to work on
j o b
thieves
t or f
legacy
i hate poems that rhyme
ant hill
continued
hot dogs and valium
ego
nonsense
day 6
ass munch
guilty
dirt and ash
found
bullshit
seize this
a buck a day
love letters
captain
welfare
dream 4836
vociferous baseball
september dusk
load and lock
sky
touch of blood
share
struggle
what
if
writers
dream
green
fence line
pray for me Stevie Ray
puss

12/24/02 9:55 AM – Carrizal

growth

it is quiet
the world has slipped
off the slope of my life
dripping
from the edge

it's out there
somewhere in the darkness
the Christmas lights and people

in the absence of it all
i search the soundness of
my courage
my solitude
my emptiness
but this i have chosen
so i drift into
the silence of the desert
waiting for a sound
a word
a wind
a whistle

a half moon in a
cloudless sky
ignites the valley before me
with every step i speak my life
my voice coarse gentle strong

i reach for God
for love
for truth

the thorns are cold and brittle
they stick deep in my flesh and burn
it hurts right now

i must be growing

salt cedar

i know
what you feel as
i cut you down at the knees

you're no good
you do not mesh
you soak up water
like i do
whiskey

alone in a crowd
half dead
dying in sun
growing in shadow

it's just your way
but your way
is not wanted here
you are forbidden
you and your gluttonous thirst for life

and the teeth of my saw
cut through your bones
poison poured into your open wounds

i step over your
dead limbs
and gulp water
from a plastic bottle
as the thunderhead
rolls in

trying

spring is coming strong tonight
it gathers in the mountains
rolls across the open plains
up the hills
through my windows

mustard weed bends
through moonlit bones
cedar posts burn in the stove
the flags pop in the wind

the moon is a ball of butter
we're all waiting for the wind to lay down
that's when the night comes alive
deer
antelope
coyotes
and a million million bunnies
they fuck like rabbits

i piss in the dirt
then the wolf
then the shepherd
then we go in
and eat meat
and i put the last log on the fire
it glows orange inside
and blue outside

the animals sleep
the flames are warm and pretty
a picture show of my youth
it's mostly blank
empty or hiding

maybe i know what i know
but i'm still trying
to understand

fade

it's not that you don't
say anything particularly
profound
or that i'm uninterested
in most of what you say
or the fact that
i can never recall
anything
from our conversations

it's that i was
fading away

i'm sorry
but i fade on
everyone

4/9/04 8:51 AM – the warsh

atheists

must be
the loneliest people

what an empty corner
in which to turn
filled with nothing

but the corner
still exists
so does
the nothing

cogitating on this particular
conundrum is no different
than trying to figure out people

which is really
no different
than watching
a cow
simultaneously
walk and shit

selfish

after a week of rain
there's finally
a shadow
on the ground

i see it
round and breezy
beneath a mulberry tree

i didn't
miss them
while they were gone
but now that they're here

i'll be
looking
for them

interstice

religion
divides
much more
than
faith
unites

this
unfortunately
will
end the world

first

my heroes
they're all dead
or they're dying
living like hell fired
mustangs
or decaying
in old crusty smiles

preacher says

live today as though
it were my last
tomorrow
is an uncertainty
at best

i buy it all
every minuscule molecule

so i sit here
in complete solitude
writing words
few will
ever
see
and
none
will
ever
truly
care for

but my fire
burns well

my afternoon wine
runs dry
and steady

my animals sleep
solid
the morning cattle wore them out

me too
but that sleep
escapes me

like with a beautiful woman
i've blown it
and too quickly
told her
how i loved her so

now i must beg
just for her
to look my way

foolish
and petty
shameful
and shitty
and forever
and did i say ridiculously
pussyish

so good luck in hell

and
i'll see you
tomorrow
or
never

which ever
comes first

hostage

there are no
green lights
here

it seems as if
i haven't seen
a green light
in years

in town
we have
a
red light

it's to remind us to slow down
be sane
give someone the honor
say hello to seldom seen folks

if that red light
ever stopped flashing
i'd have to find a new home
because there'd be green beneath it
which means
the red doesn't just stop you
it holds you hostage

3/1/4 11:55 PM - the warsh

out

things are great

power out
water out
food out
heat out

blacked out

out of flushes
out of ice
out of mind

out of nothing
really

pie

one time
i learned
the quadratic formula
and
used letters in equations
even solutions

now
i wonder
why
i ever did such
absurd
things

fuck me

i don't want to fuck the women
who want to fuck me

their confusion
confuses me
oh
the enigmas of life

but really
it's because they're not the ones

the one

that one's
come
and
gone

and that
was that

plenty

i will
never
walk on eggshells
not for anyone
ever

if i do
bring a frying pan
there'll be a trail of scrambled eggs
for eternity
before and after me

it would be a pleasurable job
for one who enjoys the outdoors

my outside is mighty
and quiet and wild and sleepy
more animals than people
and the people
are good
and decent
and tough and honest

words
are more than
words

they are few and straight
i wish for more
but it's too proud a gesture
its burden is soul bearing integrity

there is trust in the mountains
the trail is rugged and mean
sometimes
there is no trail
though some still manage
to find their way
and the scars
are sewn in their
word
it's simpler that way

time is appreciated
nothing goes to waste
room for everyone
but everyone's not here
they're out in the noise
and light
and dirty
swollen rain

i wonder if they know

i know they wonder
i did
not anymore
never again
ever

i like
sausage and bacon
with my eggs
sunny and runny

so bring plenty

110 percent

sometimes
you just
have to admit
that you
completely
suck shit
at whatever
ridiculously
simple
thing
it is
you think
you're trying
to do

so go drink
a lot
don't talk to any idiots
piss outside
sleep outside with the dog
smoke pot incessantly
kill a wild animal
and share it with them dogs too

do something dangerous
something good
something that could
kill you

then
when you're not
too busy doing
all that stuff

give it another
whirl

it might be
easier this time

recovery

mine is coming on
but i'm splitting myself at the legs
every side burns
and
my hands shake
in the mornings

sometimes my legs tremble
sometimes i vomit down the mountainside
sometimes i just stay stoned

and when the pain begins to wear
i look away
out beyond it all
and wonder if this process
isn't really death
in recovery's clothing

same

sometimes
i just get tired of searching
i don't know where to look anymore
everyone found it
except poor old me

it just seems this way
it's just weakness
it's natural imperfection

i need music in my soul
Mozart had a way of stringing it together
and he was just the same
as the rest of us

but much much better

early

i called a friend
early this morning

he answered the phone
i would never do this

he has a swollen leg
maybe a clot

and as my early spring morning
broke into birdsong
whispering farewell to the great quiet

he was a thousand miles away
tucking his starched shirt in
headed to his office
then the doctor's
then to everywhere

stoned sleepless
sitting there
soaking in the fire of
dusk down the mountainside

i was hoping
and pleading mercy
and drinking cold Lone Star beer
and even
imagining the dreadful weight
of his absence

but that's not why i called

eight

they call it
the desert
because there is
little water
no water

but sometimes
there is fast
strong death water

it is country
only for the hearty
the stubborn
the brave
the free

it sticks and burns and bites
and snows
and siroccos
rip across the prairies

dust is life
it is everywhere
and unseen

today
i dug a hole in the ground
then planted a thornless Mesquite
we broke away rock for hours
and barrowed the rubble to the
roadside

it's troubling to me
how fewer things
become sacred
at 8 dollars an hour

jogging

in town
i saw a couple
jogging
a baby or 2
in the 3 wheel stroller jogger tent

the couple wore exercise clothing
light
bright
right

i was
going to write a
poem
about them

instead

i'm
going to ride
a horse

those
are my 2 choices

life
is fair
today

good

i'm essentially useless
by nature

but when i work at it
i'm really good

juice

it's 6 in the morning
and i'm riding
the tall side of a blaring high
sitting around
mainlining
trumpet juice

too hung over
to sleep

thinking of funny people
things they do that amaze me
that melt my imagination
into a fresh flow
that streams heavy and warm
making me smile
in my little world

life flies by
in the whistle of a train

it just keeps
passing through

just brushing by
my room
of blue light and wolf dream

i dare
dread the day
it ever stops
for me

7.7.7. 7:57pm - warsh

Welch's

i'm not very good
at grocery shopping

i walk in
unprepared
drunk
high

i can find
the beer
meat
and tortillas
the rest
is just a somnolent
hell
of solicitation and tasty chemicals

then
my basket
pulls down
heavy
on my arm
and the walls
collapse

sometimes
i can
make it to the end
by reaching in the cooler for a bag of ice

and sometimes
like last time
i drop the basket
and drive away
trying to stay between the lines
and console
the confused eyes
of my old
backseat dog

years

it's happened
twice
this year

when writing a hot check

i pause

lean out of the fog
and
ask the clerk

what year is it

things are coming along
real fine

not what i expected
but i never expected
much

6.3.00 / 11:30 AM – randall's pharmacy (bingle location)

waiting

she comes hobbling in
her flip-flops flip-flopping

pregnant
fat

both

my prescription ready yet

about 30 minutes mam

she waddles away in her denim cut-offs
flapping flip-flops and cauliflower thighs

wait
she's not done yet

where the cigarettes at

between the a and the t
you fucking wart hog

pardon

where the cigarettes at

the pretty clerk directs her
to the other end of the store

she flops away
without a word

lovely
i thought

welcome

my
survival advice
to desert newcomers

is

should you get
bit
by a rattlesnake
immediately
remove your cock ring

unctuous dick

slick is what he is
ice on oil
on lard
on bile
on bacon grease

you'll hear what you want
you'll hear everything and everything
excuses mainly

but that's him
that's poor old him
poor
poor
him

and fault
and blame
and self pity
these are lies
with which he juggles
and songs
which along side
he sings

my advice

look at that
sorry fuck
in the mirror

point your
fat finger
at his fat face

apologize to the world

forgive the lost
embrace the present
and carry on

there are too many things
behind life

and monkeys
belong in trees

backs are for carrying
what others can not
and more so
for what they can

and mercy is man's greatest strength

so let it go
and
fly
fly
fly away on a tender song

out here

my teeth are rotting
there's cat shit on the floor
i'm hungover
thirsty
sober
and dirty

puppy naps
and dog naps
are two different things

cat naps are eternal

summer is here now
i want to swim
and fish
and drink cold beers
but i live in the high desert
water is scarce
but pure

i feed and water cows
to keep them alive
until we kill and eat and wear them

i've never injected heroin
because i know it's just right for me

but the water in the tanks
is warming
soon
i'll be floating in the
sun circled mountains
beer and birds and the Talking Thunderbird Blues

sometimes i read about the world
from space it looks so tranquil
yet the papers tell a different story

it's almost here
sunsets in a water trough

and when i'm finished

peeling away
the tiny black leaches
from my scrotum

i'll feed the puppy
the dogs
the cats
pour a stiff whiskey
light a late night fire
scribble some confusion
thank God for my blessings
and
wonder
why
here
in this majestic place
in its immense silence
in its ethereal warmth
in its place outside the world
i still think of killing myself

Paco

Paco makes grills
actually he puts the wheels on the bar-b-q pit frames
he does it 5 days a weeks
an average of 250
wheeled frames
per day
by Paco
that's 13000 rolling pits a year

without Paco
they'd have to be drug around
that would leave ruts
and inappropriate places to grill

Paco doesn't mind
the factory is clean
his kids still love him
and even though most of his friends
are dead
or in jail
he still
gets a thrill out of making
those wheel less grills
roll

depression

is great
barren will
unable to attain
true will
again

twenty

when i was 20
i crossed a snow covered street in Chicago
it was cold
i was cold
and hungry
and broke

suddenly
there in the dirty slush
appeared a wet 20 dollar bill

i reached down
and snatched it up
without breaking stride

inside my apartment
i dried the bill on the furnace
i looked at it as it dried
and felt so damn lucky

then
i ran back into the street
down to where i'd found the 20

it was a lime green bus
that slammed into the shit puddle of icy mud slush

i was covered in street feces
and i was colder now

i'd been shat upon
by myself
and it only cost me
20 bucks

hell

sometimes
when i'm drunk and stoned
i think of the day
my guardian angels
come to me
and ask

what do we do

give em hell

and they do
and i do
and it all goes God's way

fool's luck

i've been
given
two
second chances
at life

two

some people get one
some people get none

so far
i got two

that's pretty good

why me
is
beyond me

and other than
completely
fucking up
both chances

i must say
i've had a
grand time
all
the blessed
while

care

most of you
i don't like

i don't hate you
really
i just
don't want to know you

this has always been
hard
for the women
that i've dated
and married

there was no understanding in them
and i can
and
can not
understand that

in-laws
don't
interest me

if i wanted
to date the
whole world
i'd a bought
a fucking station wagon

who's the asshole who said
it wasn't human to be alone
i find happiness
there
my cat
between the keyboard
and the monitor
my wolf asleep at my feet
lamp light
fans and scotch

a party
would be like
fucking
a cadaver
right now
any now

it's okay
not
to include me
i'd prefer it that way
then
i don't have to waste my time
making up
some horseshit excuse
for why i wasn't there
i'd be
forced to lie
and
i don't lie
often

i was here
because i knew
i had a choice

i would've come
to your place
but i simply
didn't want to

take care

8/10/2005 12:20 PM – mckoetting

my marriage

was
like a
bad dream
with
big tits

goats

everything's good
when you got
nothing better

do you mind if i
sleep on your floor tonight

you gonna eat
the rest of them
fries

mind if i grab a beer
a cigarette
a hit off that joint

could you give me a ride
sorry
need another one
and endless others

just take the truck
take it and fuck it up
take it and just keep going

i'm a goat roper
not a cowboy
definitely
not a cowboy

looky here

don't fuck your sister
don't make bad music
don't listen to it either
don't let some one
shit in your mouth
just so you can
get on the internet
don't fuck animals
for any reason
even dead ones
never harm a child
or a woman
or anyone
less than
your own match
in self defense
leave dead people alone
mind your own business
and help someone
other than yourself
then keep doing it

can't you see

being petty is
a fool's purpose

my dying dog

won't die
she doesn't want to
she falls
because her hips have eroded
she walks into walls
because she can't see them
she wets her chair
and she sleeps a lot because
she needs to rest

she can't see
the trail of shit following
behind her
but she knows it's there
i see the shame
in her eyes
but it's okay
i'm here
just as she has been
since six weeks

that was
14 years ago

if she was human
she'd be 98 years old
and dead

if she was human
i would have
put her down
a long time ago

curious

i don't know which
is more exhausting
doing something
or doing nothing

it seems as though
it takes less time
to do something
and more time to do nothing

also
it appears to me
that there are plenty of folks
doing something

and crowds are for concerts
hell
and
free giveaways

it is plausible
though
that one can
drink
fuck
smoke
shit
sleep
eat brisket tacos
gas station corn dogs
and still do nothing

i'm off to nap
on a bed of excuses

that's doing something and nothing

curious

rad

Hey Rad? You there man? You still wit me bro?

I'm still here, bubba.

You know I got to thinkin about it the other day. You know, Rad, I just got to thinkin on it. Hey Rad? Let me ask you this right quick. On a scale of one to ten, what would you say the last couple days of your life have been like, man. What do you think it's been like? I'm really serious, Rad, how about it, baby?

Eleven. You ask me that every time we talk.

Eleven! Rad, that's off the charts, baby! Off the charts! That's what I'm talking A-bout baby!

He never hears me tell him that he does this every time. So I sit silently, imagining him screaming "off the charts" all over the office waving the phone and kicking his feet the way he does.

Hey Rad, You still there?

Yessir.

I'm lovin it, Rad! Eleven! That's my boy! That's doin it, man! I love it! Just love it, Rad! Hey Rad, I was gonna tell you somethin, man. You know, I got to thinkin on it the other day, you know, all this stuff about death and death and death. And you know somethin, Rad? I decided somethin. You know all this being angry at people and stress and stuff. It ain't worth it. What's the point, Rad? Ya know what I mean, Rad? It's bullshit, man. So I decided somethin, Rad, I decided I'm gonna go ahead and kick it up a couple of notches. You know what I mean? I'm gonna kick that sumbitch up a couple notches. You with me, Rad?

I'm *always* with you.

a baseball thing

at 39 years of age
i had to quit
my 8 dollar an hour
landscaping job
because my boss
didn't like
getting his ass patted

i guess
in that line of work
there's no
ass
in team

church clothes

i used to wear a
tie and suit
every day

i paid lots of money
for those
ties and suits

when i wore them
i looked really hot

it's true

because
i was hot
and not worth a shit

warning

my lighter says flammable
my insecticides say deadly
my mother says be careful
my liquor bottles say drink responsibly
even on the cases

the doctor says eat
the doctor says don't drink
the doctor says pot's a depressant
he's also my dealer

they're everywhere

i'm here by choice
by grace
one way or another

why i am such a pussy

it's too hot
or cold
or sunny
but it never rains

i didn't sleep
i overslept
my butt hurts

i got lost
i forgot
i've got jock itch

it's already 3 pm
the pills make me sleepy
and there's war on tv

i'll lay back
pull my hat over my eyes
a quick power nap

then
maybe
write a while
or help clean up
and it's 6 pm

the game is on in an hour
the dogs need fed
it's time for a scotch

i'm hung over
i'm stoned
looks like it may rain this evening

control

if i could
control
life
they'd call me
God
instead of asshole

things to work on

joy
is what i miss
the most

this world has
never
quite
made sense
to me

i smiled as a child
because i wasn't trying
to understand it

i'm not a child
anymore

i smile when
i'm sideways
or when i see
innocence
without shame
or when someone
gets hit in the nuts
with
a golf ball

actually then
i laugh hard
real hard

j o b

some people have jobs
because they want them

some have jobs because
they're supposed to

some because they
don't have a choice

some people can
hold a job for 27 years

some people can't
hold a job for 27 minutes

some people have jobs
just to get away
from their soul mate

i don't have a job
because
i can't stand people dumber than myself
telling me what to do

jimmy wichard
says

if you work
for jimmy
you work hard

too many jimmies
live on this planet

i think i'll
stay on
my side
of the world

thieves

these folks from out of town
were awfully friendly to me
when they needed me to work for them

we pay a hundred dollars a day
twelve hours a day
6 days a week

i'm just a dumb fuck
lucky
to have a job offer

i hadn't done shit my entire life

not until i walked up to you
and knew for certain
my time was wasted

a hundred a day
is hardly 70 after all dues
that's just over
5 bucks an hour

okay
that sounds terrible
i won't take it

then things went missing
in the middle of the night
and i was at the top of the shit list

didn't find out until a week or so later
but it lit a charge in me
that made me want to
tear down the world

i don't steal

if it ain't mine
it stays that a way
that's final

falsely accused of stealing

is a terrible feeling

but for some reason
paying a man
5 dollars an hour
ain't

even if he turns you down
hell
blame the sorry bastard anyway

we're the world
he's nothing

nothing but a fucking thief

9/12/2006 8:06 AM –rnp

t or f

a friend of mine
wrote a story
mused somewhat
by me

at first
i thought
he was joking

then it came out
his second book

i saw him
one night in a bar in town
sweet Joe Ely sang from his heart
Guy Clark gave us a whirl
Butch Hancock made me cry
and Terry Allen played hard
and drank hard
and made everyone
smile and sway

as per usual
we were both drunk
he grabbed me by the arm
and told me

go get the fuckin book
if you ain't got the
12 bucks
tell them sumbitches
to charge it to me

i bought the book
i read the stories
i read his poems
each one taking me away from myself
running off to a swampy warmth
of cajun delicacies
holding in the murky waters
of his memory
and suddenly
i understand

that drunk asshole
has more free time
than i do
and i don't even have
a fucking job

though
i must say
i don't believe i have
ever
mused before
but now
that i have

it feels like
the dew drying
on the late summer purple
of the Mexican feather grass
then proudly leaning up
into this morning's
fine mountain sunshine

soon
they'll be
fine and straight

unlike myself

i'll stay stoned
and lost
occasionally
wishing
i had half
the courage
of my
kind friend

legacy

just to top
her husband

she's gonna have to get
buttfucked by her brother
in the oval office

i don't think
she has a choice

i hate poems that rhyme

need
greed

ant hill

so you decided to kill us all last night
you decided we would all go with you

everything's on you

you
that's why
i will never live in an apartment again
or a high rise
or a duplex
or a garage apartment
or anything within a flame's
reach of some jack off
passing out
with a hot dog up his ass
and a cigarette in his mouth

an infamously bad neighbor myself
the usual atmosphere
not suitable
for young humans

but i only put hot dogs in my mouth
and i don't smoke cigarettes

as a wise dead friend
once said

i just smoke pot
cigarettes'll kill ya

he was shot in the heart by the police
died wearing nothing but a revolver
and boxer shorts

those damn cigarettes
and ants

i figure the further from the hill
you are
the better the view when it falls

cheap seats
for the armageddon

and when the dust clears and flames die
i can say

that's why

do you understand now

now what do i do

who's going to fuck up everything for me

like concerts and footballs games
and dinners and silent moments
and movie houses
and funerals too

and there's no answer
and no ants
and nothing left for me to blame
all because some jack off
couldn't find a hot dog
big enough for his fat ass
so he lit up the world
and smoked us all away

continued

how many
excuses
are there

i thought
for sure
i'd run out
by now

hot dogs and valium

i just took
one

a big blue one

with a bottle
of Texas red wine
a bowl
of chili
2 hot dogs
no bread

across the room
those Siamese eyes
are drooping

i can't hear his purr
because the fan
cuts fast
through the hot air

hot air
hot wind
hot dogs and valium

life is just too damn fair sometimes

i'm off to purr now

ego

some are so big
they kill millions
without remorse

they don't feel guilt
nothing of it

they don't understand
humankind
they don't hold it
as they should
like a small bird
shaking in the cradle
of your hands

though
i must admit

i'm about
ninety percent
asshole
and ten percent
cock

that's cock
in the sorry lazy chickenshit asshole
sort of way

but i don't kill people
nor do i necessarily like them
especially the egotists

they're stone casters
and
often enough
i'm everything but different

nonsense

fools delight in pettiness

it's fear for the frightened
and stones for the martyred

it's a sick necessity
for the insecure
the unsure
the weak

the child hugs
just weren't there

well
i say hug
my big fat sweaty cock

quit complaining
it's boring
it's depressing
it's incessant
and a strangely embarrassing
unnecessary fiasco in which to participate

i'm trying to live
i'm after what's inside me
even if it's nothing

stay out of my way
take the self pity with you
give it to someone who needs it

but you might ought to know
crutches can only carry so much
until they crumble
beneath the weight
of their own worn weathered worthlessness

day 6

dear God

You did great
until day six

sincerely

bfk

ass munch

she got the rust
off the old
wagon wheel

that's for sure

guilty

why do i
pay
for insurance
when there really is none
it's paper wasted
covered in lies

why do i
pay
to be advertised to on tv

why do people
pay
taxes
at years end
when they already
pay tax
every time they piss

i pay tax on the
tv service that
i've already paid for
just to be
incessantly hassled by
a bunch of delusional
soulless pigs

it's endless and growing
and never stopping

because i'm
just lazy
and
just stupid
enough
to allow it

dirt and ash

where is the old world

where is all the hell
that made me crazy

i wonder if it's still there
or
if it died the death
i saw coming

if not
let it die now
let the rain fall
the evil drown
the cactus flowers blossom
let fire burn away the sin
and kill the chaos
and let them live
only to hear the silence of the end

this is where we'll start
greedless
from the wet dirt and ash

found

there's
nothing
close to
solitude

it is the furthest
one will ever see
into
the promises of the soul

and should you
ever
turn away
the quiet
that once drowned you
will
haunt your dreams
light or dark
and make you
beg
for its return

the truth
is in the
silence

that's where
it
found me

bullshit

insurance
how can a man sell
stacks of swiss cheese paper and sleep

campaign promises
whatever you just said
bite me

technicalities
these are the death holes of justice

and the death tax
dying ain't free ya know

the designated hitter
the intentional walk
most advertisements
especially those mail order rubber pussies
what a short shelf life
those pieces of shit have

most of what cascades
from the blathering
mouth of the human race
and everything i will ever say

yesterday i photographed a black bull shitting

he snorted at me
and slung about his slobber
i took a few photos
then he walked away
his tail swatting the flies

real bulls give real shit
they don't take it

maybe instead of my
regular nine o'clocker
i'll drop a calf

seize this

i have
many
things to do

but i'm more interested
in thinking about
doing these things
than actually
doing them

i imagine myself
successfully completing
each task
without complication

which is completely asinine

a buck a day

that's it
that's all it amounts to
it's that simple
a buck a day

a buck a day
gets you
everything you need in life

happiness and sunshine
and straight white smiles
and straight white people
doing straight white things

and i don't understand
why we don't grow
horns
on our heads
and burn the world down

love letters

every once in a while
i'll organize
the papers
on my writing table
stories here
poems there
articles here
rants there

then i'll stack my bills
on top of one another
then stack the late notices
on top of them
then stack the
termination notices
on top of them
then stack the
collection notices
on top of them

then the letters from the attorneys

sometimes
they reach over a foot high
and fall over
i stack them up again
this time in order of size
biggest on bottom
smallest on top
it makes a nice structure
and lends a legitimate use to the paper
then i'll stare at the stack
for a few minutes
as though it were a work of art
then i'll drink red wine
and scratch my cat's neck
then i'll go to bed
and dream
that someone
keeps sending me
love letters

captain

right now
and most likely
for some time to come
i fucking rule

how i made it this far
is a question only for God

i've decided that i am the fucking captain
simply because
i got my money back
from a whore's pimp
because my dick is too big

it's a long story

now i'm drinking whiskey
alone in the Texas desert
a cold night
a big ranch
a black bull
a cow with her retarded calf
a wolf killing and eating jack rabbits
a black and white cat with worms
all the cats with worms
all the animals with worms

if only there were a fishing hole nearby
for the ol captain

welfare

when i was on unemployment
it was called t e c
Texas employment commission

then they changed the name to
t w c
Texas workforce commission

boy that really helped

dream 4836

after all this time
you finally spoke to me
i hated your tone of friendship
it was ingenuous
only necessary
considering

but the two city men with you
were goodhearted and helped me
unload the carcass
in return for the freedom you received
lost
stranded far away from your elements
scared dark and cold

you were just friends
but too close for my comfort
your teasing them made everyone laugh
but not me
i was torn
busy with the carve of my kill
wishing i had never found you there dying

and you never thanked me
for the food or warmth of the fire
nor the shelter
nor the wine

so i empathized with Jesus Christ
and awoke into the morning light
feeling my solitude had been raped and scarred

outside my cabin
the good dry air
filled my lungs with promise
and the sad thought of you faded away
into the mountains

vociferous baseball

i am ill in doubt
something lives within me
it's small
but mean
and eats me inside without my consent

self doubt beads on my skin
seeping up like fever water
until i flow outside the ache in my bones
and long to kill the sick man in my home
because
he is weak
he is lost
he is dust on the sheets
he is without his ways

let him crawl into the desert and die

let the turkey vultures
pick beneath his ribs
and the sun
dry his skin to a crisp pelt
brittle bones spent of marrow

let him lie hollow
on the roadside

his tongue
curled dry in the sand

let him
venture on
and find
his peace

september dusk

cotton birds of purple and orange
suspend in formation over the Chinatis
as the fireball drops away
warming the slopes beyond my sight

i've come up from the canyon to see you off until morning
the breeze is cool steady and colorful
Greasewood and Mesquite dance in relief
and the Cottonwoods gather their time of rest

i still can't believe you're gone
i feel a great loss
as though God has left for a while

and off in the distance
the bitter sweetness of the heaping Sierras
and the pyramid they call Cerro Baludo

i stand on the ancient ocean floor
now relieved of its burden
sleeping gently
beneath the clean hues of september dusk

the blues are still of the deepest seas
it's perfect in every way
and
there is
nothing here but
you and me

load and lock

rain fell last night. i slept hard. dead. buried in the trenches of a dream. i was back in the city. walmart. the parking lot was a war zone. guns. fire. heavy artillery. gang against gang and shoppers casually pushing their loaded carts to their cars. a young blonde girl loads children's toys into her trunk. i watch from just outside the glass exit doors. her white t-shirt bursts. she falls to the pavement. dead. blue volvo sedan. blonde dead girl. i go to get her. "get your white ass outta here, cracker boy!" i look at them. kids. the girl's body heavy in my arms. smoke. whining bullets and she's the only one dead. i take her inside the store and lay her down on a display bed.

home décor department

i place a pillow under her head. white teeth painted blood red. a floral patterned bedspread atop 50-50 sheets i pull just above her shoulders. i kiss her pale forehead. warm lips. cold skin. other shoppers stop and laugh as though i've molested one of the store's mannequins.

sporting goods department

there is no "associate." i smash the glass gun case. with an AR-15 and several boxes of ammunition i make my way to the roof. i load and lock. anyone who locks and loads is doing it wrong. at the edge of the roof the chaos is almost beautiful and patriotic. someone digs through the trunk of the dead girl's volvo. i fire one shot. the backside of his head explodes away. he falls into the trunk. all is silent. all. through the smoke a light finds me standing there, gun in hand. five shots into the light and it's out. i walk thirty paces down the rooftop. as i watch, the spot from where i shot is blown to rubble and dust. one large blast. they can't see me, but i can see them. all of them. scattering beneath the parking lot lights. ants caught in the rain. "cracker boy shot g-spot!" another kid. he fell with a bullet through his throat. no one tried to help him. cowards. boys playing men. i shot everyone i could see. dead weight thumped the concrete as though the sky was raining wet bags of shit. departing shoppers bent over the bodies. pulled bloody wads of cash from their pockets. took jewelry from necks and fingers and ears (no nose rings). wore them with pride. returned to the store. more shopping. "fuck!" i was disappointed. "i'm gonna have to slaughter the whole lot."

electronics department

i turned off every device that made a noise. there were lots of devices. on the bottom shelf a small black and white television. i turned on the baseball game. A's at Fenway. tied 1-1. extra innings. i sat Indian style on the dirty tile floor. Trot went yard in the bottom of the eleventh. game over. television off.

home décor department

tired. i crawl in bed with the dead girl. the rifle with me. beneath the 50-50. i drape a lock of her hair over my eyes. scents of berries and soap and blood. as i dozed i knew that even one percent of polyester against my skin would make me sweat.

i woke soaked. the ground just outside the rock wall of the Carrizal was white with salt pulled up from the rain. it was the storm rolling in that i had wanted to see. the rain had stopped. no one was dead. there was no one to die, except me. i drug myself inside, shivering while i stoked the fire. i rested my head on my wet boots. the fire cracked and popped and hissed. i finished my scotch and rain. day was breaking. on the concrete floor i slept next to the fire.

let them slaughter themselves

that's their world

not mine

sky

i saw it all
my sky was a boil of burning clouds
yellow lightning
multiple rainbows

i saw it all
the beginning
the end

you didn't
you saw nothing
blinded
like a mule a front a wagon

i don't pity you though
i've told you of its magnificence
but you don't know

i hope you never will
the sky doesn't deserve
your arrogance
give it to those who do
your friends
your padded walls
your hands to hold and tell you
what you want to hear

and in a windy pasture at dusk
i reach skyward with an iron pipe
wondering
if my eyes would plunge from their sockets
should i be lucky enough
to be struck by the pulse of God

will smoke rise up from my corpse
i hoped
but it didn't happen
and now i'm home

but i was there
in the middle of the Fury
in the center of His might
inside the equinox of life and death

and He let me go

and now i have
the memories
and the wishes
that all evil
be fired upon by thunderbolts
and pissed upon
by wet cattle
and the sorrel gelding
beneath my saddle
at dusk

touch of blood

i have gone far away
to live quietly beneath the great sky
awaiting the birth of me
without you

i sleep by the fire
a quilt woven in stars
lulling in the call of the coyotes
yet you have emerged
in this vast land
that holds no other man

your trespass has broken my patience
it falls away like a boulder from the mountain

your taunting me has grown violent
and from your vile deeds i bleed
this was well deserved
once
but being here has changed me
for often
i kill to live
this you'd soon learn
blood down your sandstone skin

i won't let you kill me anymore
i want nothing more of it

so i force myself out of the darkness
and into the morning haze allay in the valley

stoking the coals back to flame
your bitter words deceased
your blood never there

but my wounds still seep
following me like the curious wolf
the phantom in the brush behind me
licking away the taste of meat from my face as i sleep

share

single malt scotch
and french toast
with mesquite bean jelly
makes an exquisite breakfast
lunch
and dinner

dust covers everything inside the house
the storm come through yesterday
got the place good

nothing like
trying to do something
you don't want to do

so don't waste the time

ain't got nothing to say
don't give a shit neither

if someone does
good for them
and
if someone doesn't
fine too

i wish them all luck
and hope they will all feast together
on a rotten rhinoceros
hemorrhoid or nut

fucking frogs

struggle

it's not easy
this cling to life
this day of rainless clouds
this confusing sorrow
clenching me
in its teeth

my blood drains
my spirit dropped on the ground
dead on its belly
a roving grizzly
shot in the back of the head

the silence that follows
a majestic death
is uneasy

and a world
without reason
is no different
than
reason
without a world

but my life
was never mine
anyway

still
that doesn't make
today any easier

7.9.5 7:01 pm - mccabe

what

it is the generation
which does not heed
its own bloody history
that will perish
in evil and flame and chaos

i trust that
someone
somewhere out there
is jotting
this down

if

Scotty
died yesterday

truck tire
split him in two

don't seem right
sometimes

and
what ifs

there ain't none

good night

writers

one time
i was so desperate for an excuse
i actually told someone
that i had been unable
to submit any of my work lately
because the self adhesive on the back of my stamps
had dried up

a writer hisself
he laughed

that's one of the best i've ever heard
i gotta write that down

well now you don't
drew stuart
ya asshole

dream

it's difficult
for others to understand
it doesn't make sense
and it's a shame

but if they were to ask
i'd enlist the might of free will
of poetry
nature and animals
faith and truth
stars above rattlesnakes
a horse's honor
a cowboy's word

without the pressure of people
i am faced with a
wide and wonderful
earth
which will force me
to grow into it
and touch God upon the hand
nothing
but scarred gratitude to offer

it is a choice
a bite into the bloody heart of freedom
a burden that calls me
like the wolf on the evening rim
the summer breeze over a napping cat
my horse holding solid in the shade
dogs and cattle running together
the strong smell of life in the rain

my dream
is
to run out of fear

it's out there
in the bull snot
and missing fingers
rusty horseshoes
and sun boiled bones
it's saddling and riding into a

morning's fine sunshine

i've tried to share it
but you can't give away
the unwanted

so i'll just keep quiet
and listen to them
on the other end

and i'll be content
just imagining how wonderful
it must be

or maybe
i'll film myself
nailing
one of my
balls
to a piece of wood
and post it on the internet

maybe

it's the
loneliness
that appeals to me

it leaves me
no excuses
and i sleep good
when i'm not passed out

green

my mother said we should have a
Mother to Son
talk
it had been many years
since i'd been back home

okay

first
quit sending money

no

and second
take some of it
and go to the dentist

i swigged my beer
and looked out at the sun setting over the bay

we were in a small pool of flowing water
i sat in a partially submerged chair
she sat on the edge of the pool
her feet cooling in the water
a cold beer in her hand
and her perfectly straight white teeth

no braces
no cavities
not one
ever

what's wrong with my teeth

honey they're green

i laughed and drank from my beer
she looked so concerned as i smiled
a big proud slimy green smile

oh how she loves me so

good ol green teeth

that's my new nickname
good ol green teeth
i like it mom

she smiled in defeat
and looked out at the shimmering bay

in Mexico
a dentist told me what it would cost
to chisel off the algae
and get my choppers all fixed up

todos

that's when i decided
it'd be cheaper
just to move to England

fence line

my hands are raw broken blisters
cramps clench them into peculiar shapes
i'm poked by yucca and barbed wire
blood drizzles dry
as i strip away the bark
from the staves
thinking of the longhaired fool
who laughed at the news of bees
stinging the face of his dog
left where he had chained him

loop the wire
pull and twist
cut
tighten
tuck
do it again
do it a thousand more times
do it as the sun lays soft
on the distant pastures
and the mountains
become rolling air shadows in blue dreams

and i laugh now
pushing down on the earth
to unlock the malnourished muscles
and remembering
how it was only funny to me
when the dog ran away
and smiley slapped at his scared face
and pulled at his beautiful long hair
the whole hive upon him

pray for me Stevie Ray

it was after
the fire had ashed the forest and all its homes
to smoking ruins

they came
to me
in a maroon honda civic
i saw
two
beautiful
long haired
brunettes
with snow white teeth
card sharp smiles of hope
pulling up to the Carrizal

we're lost and need a place to stay for the night

i tucked
my pistol
back in my belt

it was going to be
double trouble

pray for me Stevie Ray

i
sure need
this one

9/12/2006 7:51 AM – rnp

puss

why would anyone
ever give a fuck
what anyone else thinks

by God
have courage
my friend

strap on some
faith in Jesus
loosen up the muscles
in your butt hole
let your balls drop
out of your chest
tie them to your scrotum
if necessary

use a thick rubber band
use some bailing wire
use something

someone else
has already
suffered worse
than you
or i
ever will

go on now
get

www.ingramcontent.com/pod-product-compliance
Lightning Source LLC
LaVergne TN
LVHW091202080426
835509LV00006B/790